Michelle Payne

Squad Goals

Salamander Street

PLAYS

First published in 2021 by Salamander Street Ltd.
(info@salamanderstreet.com)

Squad Goals © Michelle Payne, 2021

ISBN: 9781914228070

Printed and bound in Great Britain

10 9 8 7 6 5 4 3 2 1

★★★★★ "an uproarious celebration of sisterhood and open-mindedness"
A Younger Theatre

★★★★★ "an energy induced, high adrenaline production"
Creative Reviews UK

★★★★ "utterly exhilarating"
The Stage

★★★★ "lively & inspiring"
Sardines Magazine

★★★★ "beautiful play about the beautiful game"
BritishTheatre.com

The first performance of *Squad Goals* was on Monday 14th September 2020 at Dagenham & Redbridge F.C.

CAST
LEXI Ellie Seaton / Lucy Aiston
MEL Holly Richard-Smith / Yasmine Gazzal
MISSY Holly Liburd / Jasmine Davis
AMANDA Tianna Sealy-Jewiss / Bessy Ewa
SHANE Jamie Corner / Joe Thompson-Oubari / Oliver Bower
MISHA Ashley Runeckles / Annie Service
SCRAPPY-DOO Charlotte Payne / Leonie Wall / Morag Davies
SHARKY Kia Brame / Jade Marvin / Morgan Sadler
ELLIE-MAE Annie Southall / Victoria Louise
ASSASSINA Giorgia Falcioni / Alice Gruden
ACTOR ASM / BOX OFFICE Pippa Conway

Directors Mia Jerome & Michelle Payne
Movement Director & Choreographer Sundeep Saini
Sound Design Nicola Chang
Lighting Design Holly Ellis
Casting Director Sydney Aldridge
Stage Management Sophia Tuffin, Natasha Harper-Smith & Emily Blaxland

Stadium Stewards Wayne Sacre, Peter Whaley, Antony Harman, John Morgan, Kelly Porter & Jason Barthram

With thanks to
Steve Thompson, Chris & Ben, Peter Freund and all at Dagenham & Redbridge Football Club, Arts Council England, Queens Theatre Hornchurch, Mercury Theatre Colchester, Helen Mumby (The Soho Agency), George Spender (Salamander Street), Chloe Nelkin PR, Rebecca Pitt, Jamie Scott Smith (West End Video), Zac Cooke Photography, George Hughes & Daniel Starmer (Huge Star Productions), Inika Organics Make Up, Kelly Jones, Gurdev & Winefride Saini, Sarah & Jeffrey Clements, Vera & Norman Dawson, The Walsh Family, Gill & Steve Payne, Albie Payne, Nicholas McLean, Tracey Childs, Antony Stuart-Hicks, Leah Harvey, Barney Hughes, Steve Hastings, Kate Hall, Charlotte Bence, Ryan McBryde, Dilek Latif, Kate Golledge, Mathew Russell, Richard Swann, Christa Harris, Sophia de Souza, Stephanie Stevens, Emily Clark, Lauren Cooper, Clara Mainardi, Antonio Ayuso, Verona Smith, Hannah Khalique-Brown, Mia Kelly and Jess Dawes.

Michelle Payne
Playwright

Michelle is a director and playwright from Essex and a 2019 recipient of the Regional Theatre Young Director Scheme working on a three month placement with the Mercury Theatre Colchester. Here she assisted Ryan McBryde on *Cinderella* and has since become one of 15 Mercury Playwrights (2020/21).

Her first play, *Orchid*, won two awards at its first outing at the Moors Theatre (Camden Fringe) in 2015 – Best New Writing & Best Actress: Michelle Payne.

Writing credits include: *Memory Box* (Winner: Mercury Monologues), *Sad About the Cows* (funded by Arts Council England at Tristan Bates Theatre).

Michelle has written and directed a number of projects at Edinburgh, Camden & Brighton Fringe Festivals as well as at VAULT festival. She won Best in Fringe for her play *Full Circle* about mental health at the Brewery Fringe Festival in 2018.

Michelle is an acting tutor for the West End Kids company where she originally trained as a teenager and also for Damien Poole Theatre Arts.

Twitter: @chellesta

Rainham Wanderers

LEXI – 17

MEL – 17

AMANDA – 17

MISSY – 19

SHANE – 19

Dagenham Daggers

MISHA – 17

SHARKY – 17

ASSASSINA – 17

SCRAPPY DOO – 17

ELLIE MAE HAGUE – 18

The casting should authentically represent the world of the story.
The actors cast should be able to represent truthfully the places the
characters say they're from.

NOTES FOR THE DIRECTOR:

The play was first written in 2019 and adapted in 2020 with a socially distanced audience in mind for a COVID-friendly performance at a football stadium.

We used pink & blue wristbands to split the audience into two teams for who they'd be supporting – these were issued at box office splitting the audience as evenly as possible.

The three opening monologues were used to travel with audiences in groups of six to their seats in the stands. This meant that the monologues were performed multiple times by the actors. However these can also happen to three groups simultaneously, or as people are collecting their tickets or waiting to go in or however else the director sees fit.

During the pre-show monologues, Amanda, Sharky & Ellie-Mae filled the 5-a-side pitch with their warm ups whilst audiences were put into their seats by Misha, Scrappy-Doo & Mel.

We set our 5-a-side pitch up in front of the away stand by laying a big patch of astroturf.

We used Actor ASMs who understudied to help the audience through the space. They took on the roles of the referee & match officials during act two.

Pre Show

Lexi's Team

I'm Mel

AUDIENCE: BLUE WRISTBANDS

LOCATION: WALK TO STANDS

CHARACTERS: MEL

MEL: Have you seen my friend Lex?

I live next door to her and she's my best friend in the whole world.

I've heard there's a scout here today. Her mum's asked me to get her but how can I drag her home when there's a scout?

It's just she's 100% the type of person to start showboating, do you know what I mean, giving it a bit of the ol' Ronaldinho, but not as good obviously. We're seventeen-year-old girls after all... And he's... Well, Ronaldinho.

So Lex and me have been best mates since we were born pretty much. I know it's annoying when people say that, but we actually were. My mum said I used to cry all the time first two months I was born and when Lex arrived I stopped. It's like I was waiting for her. But yeah, she's my next door neighbour, best friend in the world and I'm hers... And her goalkeeper. I mean not anymore, cos I can't get injured if I want to be in big west end musicals... What's your favourite musical? Yeah I wanna be in that... *(etc, etc, you don't like musicals, whaaaat? Etc etc)*.

Yeah! That's what I'm doing. I'm auditioning for drama schools and for those of you who don't know, it's crap, cos like, they're not casting for a role, they're purely judging on you. And like, listen to my accent. Daisy Ridley don't speak like this do you know what I mean?

I do love playing football though, mostly for the banter and hanging out with Lex. It'll be good to see the old school girls today too. We all went off to different colleges so it'll be good to get a bit of a reunion going...

SFX: Whistle blows

Let's find you lot some seats, unless you wanna join in?

Pre Show

Misha's Team

I'm Misha

AUDIENCE: PINK WRISTBANDS

LOCATION: WALK TO AWAY STAND

CHARACTERS: MISHA

MISHA: How do young women make their mark on the world. How much does it take for us to be taken seriously?

The male PE teacher said I was the best in my year at secondary school, even better than the boys, of course I wasn't allowed to say that out loud… In front of everyone else. Because of egos. Because of gender stereotypes. He fought for me to play on the boys team, every year. I was denied. I was met with protest. The other girls didn't care. "That's Essex for you" my mum said – "seemingly happy to allow gender stereotypes and the patriarchy to rule our lives. While you're expected to be happy getting hair extensions, boob jobs, mink eyelashes…"

But the thing is I love eyelashes. I wish I could afford extensions… But I don't wanna be the stereotype. Like, am I letting Essex down by conforming to that? I want people to see more than that, you know?

At sixth form, my mum said I should start a women's team. I tried and was told there wouldn't be enough interest. My mum said it's their loss.

She said, if you wanna do something right, you do it yourself. So here it is, a community event for women's football, here, today. And we're obviously grateful to you all for coming along to support!

My family eat, sleep and breathe football. We have a BT Sport subscription. And we're excited to share that passion with you today.

A scout from Dagenham & Redbridge women's team is with us too. Mum arranged it. It's not any of you is it? Wait, would you even tell me if you were? Well, if any of you are, I'm hoping you can make a couple of decent signings from local talent! Myself included, obviously.

Suppose I should get us all started. Feel free to take a seat in the stands if you have any injuries, or you can start warming up. A couple of stretches should sort you right out.

Pre Show

Misha's Team

I'm Scrappy

AUDIENCE: PINK WRISTBANDS

LOCATION: WALK TO STANDS

CHARACTERS: SCRAPPY DOO

SCRAPPY: Rumour has it there's a scout here today and I've made it my job to find out who it is. So is it any of you?

Ah I see how it's gonna be?

Still nothing?

Do you even know what I'm talking about?

Okay, so I trust you all. Right. So Misha's mum has organised this community day thing, to celebrate women's football. Misha's been acting bare weird lately and I think it's cos of this. Like the pressure init? She's like not wanting to hang out at weekends at the moment and I don't know why. It's just all a bit suspect. As I said, it may be the pressure. Her mum is a bit… Well. This scout from Dagenham & Redbridge women's team agreed to come down and take a look. Obviously Misha's mum asked her and decided to stage this women's football event in the hope that someone *(Misha)* gets signed. As we all know, opportunities for female footballers are few and far between. Obviously Misha will get signed, BUT I really want the best chance possible for myself, so every time you see me on the ball can we make a bit of a fuss? Clapping, cheering… A bit of "We love you Scrappy! We do" And it's funny cos my name is Scrappy-DOO. We love you scrappy – we Doo… I'm singing it with two Os. Okay I'm gonna practise now… Ready, I'll give ya a bit of Cristiano Ronaldo… One, two, three…

SCRAPPY *practises step-overs with an invisible ball.*

And she shoots and the crowd goes wild –

Gesture to crowd to go wild.

That's you lot.

Gestures again.

Yes, that's what I'm talking about –

SFX: Whistle blows

Ah! Better get a wiggle on… Here's my first chance, hope I don't get cut, right? Don't forget to cheer me on alright? Let's get you all comfy in your plastic seats! Unless you fancy a little warm up yourselves. You look like you might be alright… DROP AND GIMME 20! Just kidding.

Act 1

SCENE 1

AUDIENCE: PINK & BLUE WRISTBANDS

LOCATION: AWAY STAND

CHARACTERS: LEXI, MEL, AMANDA

Enter **LEXI** *into the stands with the audience. She mingles. Are you trialling too? etc etc.*

MISHA'S MUM V/O: Welcome to Dagenham & Redbridge Football Club for our Women's Community Football Day. You have forty-five minutes to choose your teams and get registered to play in the matches. We hope you enjoy yourself today and let's hear it for the girls!

MEL *cuts through the cheers.*

MEL: Lex!

LEXI: Did my mum send you?

MEL: No.

LEXI: Mel?

MEL: Okay yes, she said final year of A Levels, you gotta knuckle down.

LEXI: It's a strong no from me.

MEL: Lex, you make me die.

LEXI: *(impression of mum)* Lexi, no football and I mean it this time, I don't want it to be like GCSE year all over again.

MEL: GCSE year when you were trialling at Fulham.

LEXI: Init tho. And I smashed my GCSEs. She's just being bare strict.

MEL: Yet here we are.

LEXI: Too right we are, hun. I'm buzzing. You're trialling with me, right?

MEL: No.

LEXI: C'mon.

MEL: You c'mon, we should head back.

LEXI: Not in front of my new mates, Mel.

MEL: I'm scared of your mum.

LEXI: Aren't we all. And at least we'll get told-off together.

MEL: I want to be a professional dancer, what happens if I get injured?

LEXI: Goalies almost never get hurt.

MEL: Petr Cech, 2006.

LEXI: Oh but he was fine.

MEL: He wears a head brace!

LEXI: You'll be fine. I'll protect ya anyway.

MEL: What am I gonna say to your mum?

LEXI: Just turn your phone off.

MEL: I'm supposed to be bringing you home!

LEXI: Is that in your official capacity of next-door-neighbour?

MEL: You're gonna be in so much trouble.

LEXI: Next-door-neighbour, roles and responsibilities?

MEL: Stop it!

LEXI: Okay. How was college?

MEL: Lex.

LEXI: *(imitating Mel)* I just love the THEATRE. What's that song you sing? *(bad impression of Mel)* "I'm all on my own"

MEL: It's just "on my own". Not "I'm all on my own" ya weirdo.

LEXI: You still got the best voice though?

MEL: I mean yeah, there's a girl who's well jealous cos I keep getting given the top line harmony part.

LEXI: Not a clue what that means but sounds sick.

MEL: How was your day?

LEXI: Still wishing Mum had let me drop politics. I'm the only girl in the class, everyone looks at me like I'm thick when I engage. So I'm just gonna stop.

MEL: What!? No Lex! What the hell?

LEXI: No one's gonna listen to a little girl from Essex are they?

MEL: I do.

LEXI: Then you're gonna stay and trial with me?

MEL: *(to audience)* Oh my god, this girl.

LEXI: It's actually so sick of Misha to host this community football day.

MEL: Her mum organised it you know?

LEXI: Naa, what, really?

MEL: Yeah. Some "soccer mom" issues going on there.

LEXI: Wish my mum was into what I was into.

MEL: Your mum is normal and cares about you a lot.

LEXI: Misha's mum has arranged a whole day to play football!

MEL: Do you think Misha's still a bitch?

LEXI: Naa, she's well alright. You'll all meet her in a bit!

MEL: Lexi, this is the girl who punched you in the back on sports day in year 10!

LEXI: Yeah, just messing though.

MEL: Right.

LEXI: It's fine anyway, I fancy a kick around!

MEL: She still a bully at her college you reckon?

LEXI: She's probably grown out of that? Sixth form changes people, ya know

MEL: I saw Missy's car out front, she back from uni already?

LEXI: She's done freshers-week and said she missed me

MEL: Don't you wanna hang out with her instead of this?

LEXI: Naa, I'm like if you're going, can you go, so I can use your bedroom as a walk-in wardrobe

MEL: Oh my god stop!

LEXI: I've asked her to come here anyway *(to audience)* so you'll all get to meet her in a bit.

MEL: What?

LEXI: She's a nightmare! Typical big sis…

MEL: She's coming here?

LEXI: Yeah, since she didn't get to go to that soccer school in Florida, she said she fancies a game –

MEL: – Your mum really is gonna kill me.

LEXI: She's doing a law degree instead, I think it'll do her good cos she's bossy as anything.

MEL: Oi, don't call girls bossy! These are words invented by boys to stop women from being called leaders. Instead they're "bossy".

LEXI: True that. Okay, yeah, she's a born leader.

MEL: Born leader!

LEXI: Must run in the family.

MEL: Ha! You think?

LEXI: Well you're still here ain't ya? About to follow me on to the battle field… Stadium.

MEL: I do miss you being my captain.

LEXI: Yeah you were always great in secondary school! Best female goalie I know.

*Enter **AMANDA**, walks through space putting out cones etc.*

Oh my god, Amanda's here? We used to go to school with her, she's a sick player, but SO perfect at EVERYTHING she does, you know, one of those?

AMANDA: *(coyly noticing crowd)* Oh hello everyone, you're all here for our women's football celebration?

Hi Lex.

LEXI: Alright.

AMANDA: Yeah.

AMANDA *exits*

LEXI: Mel. This is gonna be the best day ever!! Playing football. With old school rivals. Are you with me or not?

Beat.

MEL: Started your UCAS yet?

LEXI: *(to audience)* UCAS, is this girl for real?

MEL: Maybe you should head back and crack on?

LEXI: Maybe you should head back and crack on.

MEL: I've done mine mate. Drama schools.

LEXI: Well, I've done mine then, football schools.

MEL: What really? The US schools?

LEXI: Not really, I can't afford them remember.

MEL: How about I get you in at Pizza Hut?

LEXI: Flipping Pizza Hut?

MEL: A year to save up!

LEXI: From a minimum wage job?

MEL: You gotta start somewhere.

LEXI: And what are you saving up for? Ballet shoes? Tickets to that musical where everyone dies and they all sing about it?

MEL: I'm saving for a car first, then drama school.

LEXI: A car?

MEL: I've managed to put a deposit down on that Skoda.

LEXI: A Skoda?

MEL: Yeah.

LEXI: A flipping Skoda?

MEL: Yes.

LEXI: I didn't know it was a Skoda.

MEL: What does that mean?

LEXI: How much is that setting you back?

MEL: £500.

LEXI: Bet it's battered init?

MEL: Yeah.

LEXI: And you can't even drive yet, ya nut.

MEL: I'm gonna do one of those intensive crash courses.

LEXI: Should they call it a crash course?

MEL: And I can pick you up and take you Lakeside whenever we want.

LEXI: A bloody Skoda, Mel.

MEL: Wait til I'm driving and sneaking you to and from training, then you'll be grateful.

LEXI: Ah! So you do want me playing football?

MEL: If you can't beat 'em, join 'em!

Wait for a cheer from the audience...

Oh, on my own then? I said, if you can't beat 'em, join 'em! Wahey!

I'll stay, cos aren't I the best female goalie you know? Your mum knows you're an absolute hurricane.

19

LEXI: An unstoppable force.

MEL: Right, I'm off to ring your mum, tell her I can't find ya! – That's acting!

Exit **MEL** *– running off.*

LEXI: She runs like such a girl…

SCENE 1 (CONT.):

I'm Lexi

AUDIENCE: PINK & BLUE WRISTBANDS

LOCATION: AWAY STAND

CHARACTERS: LEXI

LEXI: I run like a girl. I catch like a girl. I train like a girl. But not just like a girl. I do all of this as a girl. In my very female skin. My very feminine body takes everything that is difficult, like I don't know – child birth, and spits it out for all to see what we can do. Don't be afraid of us. I mean really don't be afraid of us. We are to be feared after all, and we know you pretend not to be.

I am not here to be sexualised and this is no Bend it like Beckham story. We are under-funded, under-supported, mocked, jeered, ridiculed, embarrassed and shamed because of gender. Because of our form, because of our pronoun.

I was told I couldn't support Man Utd and not because I was from Essex, but because I was a girl. Even my mum prayed for me to not be into football. "Can you wear something other than a Wayne Rooney England shirt to Auntie Jackie's wedding?" The answer was no.

I tore up our garden. I played in the rain. I snuck into the workies and had a lager shandy with my dad. We cheered and we complained.

"That was never a pen!"

And more recently, we chant –

"V.A.R! V.A.R!"

My dad did help. He did acknowledge my love for the game and understood that it wasn't going away. Yet I saw no one like me in the mainstream game. I just saw men. Men who were celebrated, idolised, paid millions of pounds and I saw HIS wages rise with every season.

Now don't get me wrong the women's game is on the up. But where was it when I was growing up? As I approach the end of my A Levels and my childhood, my chance to be a professional female footballer has faded. Where were the opportunities, the scouts… the money? I need to decide on a career path. My heart is broken that football maybe can't be it.

SFX: *Whistle blows*

Sick! That's my cue. Take a seat, I'll show you how this girl does it.

SCENE 2

Drills. Drills. Drills.

AUDIENCE: PINK & BLUE WRISTBANDS

LOCATION: AWAY STAND / 5-A-SIDE PITCH (**EXT**)

CHARACTERS: AMANDA, LEXI, MISHA, MEL, SCRAPPY DOO, SHARKY

SFX: BANG BANG *(Jessie J, Ariana Grande, Nicki Minaj)*

Opening scene consists of movement section with drills. Teaser of sound design & dance routine to come in Act 2. (includes **AMANDA, MISHA, LEXI, MEL, SCRAPPY DOO, SHARKY, ELLIE-MAE**). **SCRAPPY** *gestures to her audience members to cheer her on.*

MISHA *heads up into the stands to shout down at the girls trialling. She stops the music with a big gesture – record scratch* **SFX.**

MISHA: Drills. Drills. Drills.

That's how a girl gets good technique. You my friends. Don't have good technique.

LEXI: Are you actually joking – I do drills every day. I don't have a job so I practise/ [every day after college]

MISHA: /You don't have a job?

LEXI: Let us play with you today – You know we work hard, Misha.

MISHA: Doesn't sound like it…

LEXI: You used to play with us at secondary school, what's your problem?

MISHA: No problem.

MEL: You know it's Lexi's dream.

AMANDA: It's all our dreams though!

LEXI: Oh I see! You're threatened!

MISHA: Pfft, as if.

MEL: What's your actual reason?

MISHA: It's my team… We're oversubscribed.

LEXI: Are you kidding?

MISHA: Afraid not.

MEL: Just let us play with you today.

MISHA: Have I somehow been unclear?

Beat.

LEXI: Who wants to play with you anyway?

AMANDA: We've had 58 turn up today –

LEXI: Right –

MEL: Didn't realise so many girls round here are into football

AMANDA: With the women's game on the rise it's really taking off. We've seen loads of talented women.

MISHA: I tell ya what, get yourself some decent training and match experience – then we'll talk.

MEL: How do we get match experience?

AMANDA: By playing in matches.

LEXI: We played together all the time at school!

MISHA: You've both got talent – you're just lacking, a bit.

LEXI: What does that mean?

AMANDA: Usually means fitness.

LEXI: I do drills every day!

AMANDA: You'll never be scouted with those chicken legs. *(makes chicken noises)*

LEXI: What do you mean scouted?

MEL: C'mon Lexi.

MISHA: See you next season?

> *Beat.*

> Or with your attitudes, maybe not.

AMANDA: Hey chicken leg, you could always start your own team!

LEXI: What did you call me?

MEL: Come on, Lexi. Leave it.

> **LEXI** *storms off to the* **TERRACE STANDS**.

> Okay everyone with blue wristbands, follow me.

MEL *gestures to audience to follow* **LEXI** *to the* **TERRACE STANDS**.

> Can you go and check she's alright?

> *All audience with* **PINK** *wristbands stay in their seats.*

SCENE 3 (l)

Lexi's Team

The Idea

AUDIENCE: BLUE WRISTBANDS

LOCATION: TERRACE STAND (**EXT**)

CHARACTERS: LEXI, MEL, MISSY

LEXI: What did she mean scouted? Only boys get scouted…

MEL: Okay, I didn't wanna tell you cos I didn't wanna put any pressure on, but there's a scout watching the matches today.

LEXI: What? Scout for who?

MEL: Dagenham & Redbridge Women's!

LEXI: Why didn't you tell me!?

MEL: I didn't wanna put pressure on.

LEXI: Well now there's pressure on! We have to play today. I have to be seen!

Enter **MISSY**.

MISSY: She shoots, she…

LEXI: Gareth Southgates.

MISSY: Aren't you a little young for that reference?

LEXI: Aren't you?

MISSY: Hey, hey… what's up?

MEL: They're not letting us play with them.

MISSY: You having me on? How old are we, thirteen?

MEL: And guess what, Miss?

LEXI: A scout is here.

MISSY: Oh my god! Who for?

MEL: Dagenham & Redbridge women's.

LEXI: I have to play today.

MISSY: So why aren't you?

LEXI: Well it's obviously that, isn't it? They're not letting us play with them cos we might be picked instead.

MISSY: Absolute bitches. Let's prepare a case and take them on.

MEL: For what?

MISSY: Being nasty to my sis?

LEXI: Yeah, we'll bear that in mind if you ever graduate.

MISSY: You're just jealous I've got a career now.

LEXI: This AGAIN!?

MEL: Acting is a career.

MISSY: Don't you work in Pizza Hut?

MEL: For now!

LEXI: Quality control on a cheesy crust is your current career.

MEL: Next time you both want my freebies you can think again.

MISSY: I prefer Papa John's.

LEXI: The worst bit you know was, as we left, they shouted "why don't you start your own team".

MISSY: Who did?

MEL: – And they laughed…

LEXI: Misha did.

MEL: – and Amanda called Lex chicken leg…

LEXI: Alright, Mel!

MISSY: There's a chunky girl in my halls who would bite her own limbs off for your legs!

MEL: Rude.

MISSY: Actually. Why don't you?

LEXI: Why don't we what?

MEL: Start a team?

MISSY: And I'll play.

LEXI: Erm, no.

MISSY: I'm sad without Toni and no actual lectures yet, I could do with a distraction.

LEXI: Still no.

MEL: There ya are Lex, you said you didn't think your sis would wanna hang out with you anymore now she's going to uni.

LEXI: Fuck's sake Mel.

MISSY: Aww did you little sis?

LEXI: – No!

MEL: She did!

LEXI: – Okay yeah, but that doesn't mean I wanna take on the responsibility of starting a team just for us to hang out…

MISSY: We could all do it together. It wouldn't just be you.

MEL: Yes!

MISSY: What do you reckon?

LEXI: And you think we can actually make this happen?

MISSY: Why not?

LEXI: Will there even be any girls / round –

MEL: / – women!

LEXI: – Women round here that wanna play with us?

MISSY: We only need two more. And we have our goalie.

LEXI: We'll have to ask Misha's girls for a game.

MEL: Rather you than me.

LEXI: And you definitely wanna do this?

MISSY: Of course! I'll put a post on social media and see who from my old lot is about. We need to find people asap.

MEL: We came to Dagenham & Redbridge today to play football didn't we?

LEXI: So true!

(to audience) Right, how many of you are good at admin? I'm gonna send you with my sister to check she's actually working on this. You lot stay with me. Do any of you fancy playing? We'll do some quick drills, see if you're up to standard

Exit **MISSY** *& a few audience members.*

MEL: I'll grab us a couple of teas from Julie's, I feel like I need some sugar for this.

Exit **MEL**.

LEXI: I guess we should ask Misha for a game…

It looks like it's all kicking off over there actually… Shall we try and have a listen?

This audience overhear **AMANDA** *parting ways from* **MISHA**'s *team.*

Majority of **BLUE** *wristbands stay here and watch* **MISHA**'s **TEAM SCENE FOUR**.

SCENE 3 (II)

Misha's Team

Scrappy Do & Sharky

AUDIENCE: PINK WRISTBANDS

LOCATION: AWAY STAND (**EXT**)

CHARACTERS: SCRAPPY DOO, AMANDA, SHARKY, MISHA

    AMANDA *bumps into* **SCRAPPY-DOO** *whilst practising fitness drills.*

SCRAPPY: Do that again, I'll knock you out.

AMANDA: Oi, chill out you absolute tit.

SCRAPPY: What did you call me?

AMANDA: An absolute tit.

SCRAPPY: I live on the Heathway, you know?

AMANDA: And?

SCRAPPY: I'm crazy

SHARKY: She's crazy.

AMANDA: Who's this?

SCRAPPY: My cousin.

SHARKY: Her cousin.

SCRAPPY: She's from Halifax

SHARKY: Not the bank

SCRAPPY: Halifax, the place.

AMANDA: Nice.

SCRAPPY: Naa – It's rough.

AMANDA: Right –

SCRAPPY: I go and stay with her sometimes, and we get smashed.

SHARKY: And go mental.

AMANDA: Misha, can I have a word.

    Were these really the best we could get?

MISHA: What's wrong with them?

AMANDA: Erm –

MISHA: Sure they're a little rough around the edges…

AMANDA: A little?

MISHA: Scrappy's from my estate, we grew up together – we can't all come from nice, comfy family homes like you, Amanda. I'm giving these girls a chance.

AMANDA: I didn't realise you live on the Heathway.

SCRAPPY: What's wrong with the Heathway?

SHARKY: You slagging off my cousin's home?

AMANDA: No not at all.

MISHA: Is it a problem that I live on the Heathway, Amanda?

SCRAPPY: Who even are you?

AMANDA: I was the top goal scorer at Harris Academy Rainham.

SCRAPPY: On the girls' team?

AMANDA: Yeah.

SCRAPPY: I was on the boys team at Brittons. No one wanted to play with me cos I broke a kid's ankle. The kid was a he.

AMANDA: What the actual fuck?

SCRAPPY: Serves him right for being male, init.

SHARKY: She whatsapped me the photos. The bone popped right out.

SCRAPPY: Misha, I don't think we need her as a goal scorer you know…

MISHA: No?

SHARKY: Especially if she's gonna act like she's all that.

SCRAPPY: I have a mate –

SHARKY: Ooh yeah!

SCRAPPY: Eye-talian.

SHARKY: Tell them what they call her…

AMANDA: Who's they?

SCRAPPY: They call her "Assassina"

Whip crack.

AMANDA: Who's they?

SCRAPPY: Everyone.

SHARKY: Us.

SCRAPPY: Assassina.

SHARKY: It means murderer in in Italian.

AMANDA: Right… Misha can I have a word?

MISHA: Sure

SHARKY: She alright?

SCRAPPY: Naa, let her go.

SHARKY: Yeah, let her go.

SCRAPPY: I'll give Assassina a call then?

MISHA: Fine.

> *(to audience)* find out more about this Assassina from these two for me please and report back.

> **MISHA** & **AMANDA** *exit.*

SCENE 4 (l)

Lexi's Team

Spying

AUDIENCE: BLUE WRISTBANDS

LOCATION: STANDS (**EXT**)

CHARACTERS: AMANDA, MISHA, LEXI

(Raised voices)

AMANDA: Are those two for real?

MISHA: What do you mean?

AMANDA: Misha, you can't seriously think they're the right type of women to showcase for the scout?

MISHA: I happen to really rate them.

AMANDA: They're terrifying.

MISHA: Naa.

AMANDA: The blonde one threatened to knock me out.

MISHA: She's just passionate.

AMANDA: And they're cousins? Right little bullying double act they've got going on.

MISHA: They're my friends Mand –

AMANDA: Naa, they're too much.

MISHA: Maybe I think you're too much. You obviously are just threatened that the scout will pick all of us over you.

AMANDA: The scouts won't pick any of us if we're not playing fair.

MISHA: You're jealous!

AMANDA: What –

MISHA: Ever since I went Barking College it's like you're jealous of me or something?

AMANDA: No. You've been acting weird. You disappear at weekends. I hardly see you anymore –

MISHA: I'm with new mates.

AMANDA: That's crap. Where are you going every other Saturday and Sunday?

MISHA: That's none of your business.

AMANDA: Ah, I'm actually sick of it, Misha.

MISHA: Fine then. You're off the team

AMANDA: What? You can't do that.

MISHA: Yes I can.

AMANDA: We're supposed to be friends?

MISHA: Obviously not.

AMANDA: I'm your best player.

MISHA: If you're that good, why don't you prove it?

AMANDA: You what?

MISHA: 8.45pm – We'll have a match. See how good you actually are.

AMANDA: But, who am I gonna play with?

MISHA: Exactly.

AMANDA: What?

MISHA: 5-a-side at 8.45pm. Better get a move on putting a team together, Amanda. Unless you'd rather go home and cry about it.

AMANDA: You better believe I'll have a team.

Exit **MISHA**.

MISHA: Yeah yeah…

AMANDA: *(shouted after her.)* Who needs you anyway? I'll find a better team

(Noticing audience.) What are you lot looking at?!

LEXI: Amanda!

AMANDA: What do you want?

LEXI: Cor alright, was about to do you a favour but don't worry.

AMANDA: What?

LEXI: Naa, you're obviously not playing football any more today, so I'll see you around maybe. Come on gang…

LEXI *goes to exit with her audience.*

AMANDA: Lex. C'mon.

LEXI: Are you sorry for anything?

AMANDA: What?

LEXI: Are you sorry for anything?

AMANDA: Ah. I'm sorry I called you chicken leg!

LEXI: Yeah?

AMANDA: Yeah, I didn't mean it. I just got carried away with Misha and –

And I definitely would love to play football today! How often do we get to play for scouts?

LEXI: Okay, now we're talking. So here's the deal, Ian Beale… We wanna get scouted right? You, me & my sis…

AMANDA: Your sis?

LEXI: Yeah –

AMANDA: I thought Missy had gone off to uni?

LEXI: Yeah she did, but she's back, said she missed me too much. Anyway, with us three and Mel in goal, I reckon we've got a pretty good chance of forming a decent 5-a-side and taking on Misha for the scout… What d'ya reckon?

AMANDA: That would definitely make things round here a bit more interesting…

LEXI: So, we need to recruit one more player obviously…

AMANDA: Yeah, I'll have a think.

LEXI: We need someone good…

AMANDA: – But who doesn't take the attention away from us!

LEXI: Ha! Exactly.

AMANDA: *(to audience)* Are any of you decent players?

LEXI: And we mean like decent team players, who'll pass to us so we can show off?

AMANDA: Lex. What about a boy?

LEXI: Ha. Brilliant!

AMANDA: Because a women's team scout is never going to sign a boy.

LEXI: Amanda, you're actually a genius.

AMANDA: I did get straight 9s at GCSEs.

LEXI: Are you ever gonna drop that?

AMANDA: We need to find ourselves a man.

LEXI: First time for everything hey, Mandos?

AMANDA: Ha. First and last time you'll hear me say that.

Enter **MEL** *– passing through.*

MEL: Julie's is shut but I just got a text and that guy is here dropping off my – Oi. What's she doing here?

LEXI: Where you going?

MEL: Picking up my car.

LEXI: What? Now?

AMANDA: You've bought a car?

LEXI: Don't get too excited, it's a Skoda.

MEL: He's round the back now, I've just transferred so getting the keys and that.

LEXI: Does he like football?

MEL: What?

LEXI: Skoda man, does he like football?

MEL: Erm… I don't know. What's going on?

LEXI: Can you just ask him?

(to audience) Can you go with her and make sure he comes back with her? Amazing thank you.

AMANDA: Brilliant. So shall I go and source us some shirts?

MEL: Us?

LEXI: – Bang on!

AMANDA: And you lot can come with me.

MEL: Lex?

LEXI: She's playing for us now.

MEL: Right… *(to audience)* maybe you can explain to me on the way?

Exit **MEL** *& some audience.*

Majority of **BLUE** *wristbands follow* **AMANDA** *to the tunnel.*

SCENE 4 (II)

Lexi's Team

Socials

AUDIENCE: BLUE WRISTBANDS

LOCATION: FUNCTION ROOM (**INT**)

CHARACTERS: MISSY

MISSY: Who's got their phone on them? Great! Anyone who's got instagram, we need a social media post.

So, we need to find two more players… We need I dunno, 16-21 year old women… To join 5-a-side football team. Must be enthusiastic? What are other good characteristics? Bravery?

Asks audience.

Good at football, maybe? Okay I'm gonna do a little one-two step over trick, anyone who's got instagram you can take a cheeky boomerang, give it a hashtag … maybe Squad Goals? Tag Dagenham & Redbridge F.C. and hopefully we can recruit another player. Ready?

MISSY *demonstrates step-overs for the boomerangs.*

What's it looking like? Add a filter? Oh yeah, that's sick! Hashtag and post!

Actually…

Can I be real with you? I'm missing Toni. Toni's my… well, I don't know what she is anymore. She's gone off to play football in the US… "Soccer". Lexi didn't really like her that much, said I could do better, that it was always about Toni. Isn't it shit when little sisters are right? You feel like a failure as a big sister… She'd definitely be here playing with us today. Toni. She'd probably be the one they signed to be honest. She's lucky like that. Well talented too, but you know just a lucky person. One of those.

So her instagram is full of these girls now. American girls. Girls she's met at the school I wanted to go to… How do you compete with these stunning American girls when you're just someone from Essex? Hardly exotic or exciting is it? They've got those soft southern American accents, playing those shit instagram story games every night… and I'm just here sounding like TOWIE. She'd be mad to not have moved on I guess…

I mean it's fine. I've still got some freshers events left so maybe I'll let my hair down a bit, what do you reckon?

Sorry to get so deep on you all! Trying to hold it together. I'm glad I've made some new mates. Maybe don't tell my sister I got all soppy on ya.

Enter **MEL**.

MEL: Missy! Amanda's joining our team, so we just need one more player.

MISSY: Isn't she the one who called Lex chicken leg?

MEL: Don't ask.

MISSY: Suppose I better go check this Amanda out. Why don't you lot stay with Mel and I'll see you in a bit.

Exit **MISSY**.

MEL: I'm collecting my Skoda from a guy called Shane. He said he'd be out the back…

SCENE 4 (III)

Misha's Team

Assassina on the dog & bone

AUDIENCE: PINK WRISTBANDS

LOCATION: STANDS / TUNNEL

CHARACTERS: SCRAPPY DOO, SHARKY, MISHA

SCRAPPY: Right, so we'll get Assassina on the dog and bone.

SHARKY: Isn't it expensive to phone Italy?

SCRAPPY: She's back in the UK ain't she…

SHARKY: Oh is she?

SCRAPPY: At the Travelodge this time with her parents.

SHARKY: Travelodge?

SCRAPPY: Yeah, just over the road.

SHARKY: Over the road?

> **SHARKY** *heads over to the nearest fence to try and see if she can see* **ASSASSINA**.

SCRAPPY: Do you lot wanna come down and chat to us properly?

> **SCRAPPY** *leads audience over to* **SHARKY**, *doing high knees and football drills.*

SHARKY: So we still need one more player, any ideas?

SCRAPPY: We can do some drills while we're thinking.

SHARKY: Good idea! Physical exercise always wakes my brain up.

SCRAPPY: Come on, you lot need to help us think too… Maybe some of you might be good enough to play with us.

SHARKY: Actually I wanna practise my "running-out-the-tunnel run". I've never run out a tunnel before!

SCRAPPY: What do you mean?

SHARKY: You know like, when the players come out the tunnel and it's like mad clapping and the England band start…

SCRAPPY: Dunno if we're gonna get that at Dagenham & Redbridge mate?

SHARKY: *(to audience member)* You can practise with me! … The rest of you can we do the Great Escape theme you know how it goes? Yeah let's get that going.

The audience member & **SHARKY** *practise running out the tunnel, clapping in the direction of the stands etc etc, the audience are singing the Great Escape theme tune.*

Enter **MISHA**.

SCRAPPY: And now for the National anthem…

MISHA: What are you doing?

SHARKY: Practising our big entrances for when we get signed.

MISHA: Right. Tell me more about this high-profile Italian transfer…

SCRAPPY: So we met Assassina *(both do whip crack gesture)* last summer, didn't we?

SHARKY: I love her – she's like a legit Italian

SCRAPPY: So she was here on holiday with her family – they planned this proper cultural city break in London. Staying at the Dagenham Prem. Lucky things.

SHARKY: And I remember thinking to meself, ooh a Premier Inn, they must have money… But this year they're in the Travelodge so just goes to show money comes and money goes…

MISHA: Right…

SHARKY: She was kitted out in AC Milan clobber.

SCRAPPY: So Assassina *(whip crack)* spent every day of her cultural education in England, kicking about over Goals with me.

SHARKY: And me.

SCRAPPY: And she DM'd me this morning, she's back. Arrived last night.

And is she she good at football I hear you ask?

SHARKY: Pfft! IS SHE!?

Beat.

Actually, is she Scraps, I can't remember?

SCRAPPY: She's sick.

MISHA: The question is can she play with us?

SCRAPPY: YEP. She's in.

MISHA: Amazing.

SCRAPPY: She's heading over in a bit, she'll meet us here.

MISHA: So Scrappy, if you can go and find one of those other girls that did the drills, some one who looked half decent. Sharky can you do your goalie training over there, *(to audience)* if you lot keep an eye on Sharks, and you can head off with Scraps.

*Exit **MISHA**.*

*The audience split in half. Half with **SCRAPPY**, half with **SHARKY**.*

SCENE 5 (I)

Lexi's Team

The Skoda

AUDIENCE: BLUE WRISTBANDS

LOCATION: CAR PARK (EXT)

CHARACTERS: SHANE & MEL

SHANE: Mel? I'm looking for Mel?

MEL: Hello!

SHANE: Ah! here she is, my favourite customer.

MEL: How many Skodas are you selling?

SHANE: Ha! Just the one.

MEL: Thank you so much for this, I'm so excited to own my first car.

SHANE: And you better look after it. You see. My car is my pride and joy. It gets me from A to B but they say the car makes the man. Mercedes, Audi, Porsche… BMW. All a sign of a top class specimen. A big money man, a man who knows his worth. So I'm moving up in the world and selling my Skoda.

You see, I managed to get £500 for my old Skoda. Thanks Mel! Which means I'm now only £23,031 short of an Audi, £44,240 short of a Porsche and actually I've done some research and I'm quite taken with the Ford Mustang but I'm £35,823 short of that too. This being a real man thing is hard work.

MEL: Well I'm happy to help!

SHANE: I've parked it in Victoria Road for ya. Here's all the information, the key of course. I've received the bank transfer so it's all yours.

MEL: Oh, how am I going to get it home?

SHANE: Well, it's a mode of transport that you've paid for so –

MEL: – I haven't done my test yet…

SHANE. You don't drive?

MEL: Not yet.

SHANE: Right… I guess I could drop it off for you… where do you live?

MEL: Rainham.

SHANE: Okay, I can do that.

MEL: Nice shirt by the way,

SHANE: Thanks!

MEL: The Hammers!

SHANE: Yeah. My dad's Millwall so it's awkward, but I used to play for West Ham so lots of disagreements –

MEL: You played for West Ham!?

SHANE: Under fifteens.

MEL: You must be good?

SHANE: I was quite good, back in the day.

MEL: Do you still play?

SHANE: I haven't in a while actually.

MEL: Are you doing anything now?

SHANE: Erm…

MEL: It's just we know a team!

SHANE: Oh cool.

MEL: Let's go!

    MEL *leads audience back to the stands.*

SHANE: Football. A real man's sport. Yes mate. Imagine turning up to training in my Mustang. Living the dream.

MEL: Shane make sure no one gets lost.

SCENE 5 (II):

Lexi's Team

Gary Lewin

AUDIENCE: BLUE WRISTBANDS

LOCATION: TUNNEL

CHARACTERS: AMANDA, MISSY

AMANDA: Pulling on the number nine shirt for the first time. I'd make my mum wash it first so it smelt familiar. There's something about washing powder and football shirts. I think it was on an advert once, a muddy football shirt, washed by mum to advertise Lenor or Aerial or one of them… Just really nostalgic.

We were lucky to have girls football at school I think. My cousin said her school thought football should be for men only. My cousin said that actually she didn't mind that. My mum says my cousin is a girly girl. That basically means her favourite colour is pink and she giggles when anyone mentions Zac Efron. I think mum wishes I was a girly girl, so she could paint my nails instead of shake and vac the carpet after I've forgotten to take muddy trainers off. It's just me and mum, and Troy and Ernie. Our dogs. Ernie is mine, he's a boxer, Troy is mum's, a chihuahua. She dresses him in pink jumpers. When are humans going to realise, dogs don't want to wear clothes, however cute they look? She did get ten likes on Facebook for the pic though, and that's a lot for mums.

I used to watch Gary Lewin for England. He grew up in Essex, like us!

He started his career as a goalie, and moved into physio at nineteen, obviously we're all getting a bit old to play professionally so mum has asked me to choose a realistic career.

Today feels like it might be my last chance, you know.

Although I have been looking at these schools in America. For women to play football. Boarding schools, summer schools, for age sixteen and up, they help to get you into the colleges there. They have showcases and all sorts. Sports Recruiting USA has all the information. Then if you get into the colleges, you study for your degree and play at a high level of soccer to get noticed by pro clubs I'd want to go to the university of central Florida.

Enter **MISSY**.

But Florida seems like a million miles away right now. Miles from Mum, and Ernie and poor Troy. Who's gonna save him from elaborate costume changes if I'm not around?

MISSY: Central Florida is where Toni is.

AMANDA: So thrilled one of us got to take the chance.

MISSY: Yeah…

AMANDA: Sorry, Missy…

MISSY: No need to be sorry.

Beat.

I got the scholarship

AMANDA: What?

MISSY: Yep.

AMANDA: Why the hell haven't you gone?

MISSY: Money.

AMANDA: But you got a scholarship?

MISSY: It's the flight, it's the living out there, I didn't wanna put that financial pressure on Mum and Dad, so I lied and said I didn't get in…

AMANDA: Ah Missy that's so crap.

MISSY: I know.

AMANDA: Does Lex know?

MISSY: No, but that's why I did it.

AMANDA: What do you mean?

MISSY: If she gets in, it'll be easier for one of us to do it than both of us. She's much more driven than me anyway.

AMANDA: That's so good of you.

MISSY: Thanks. I'm sure I'll be just as happy being a lawyer anyway. I've watched so much *Suits* I'm practically qualified.

AMANDA: But you have to tell her eventually.

MISSY: Yeah maybe I will.

AMANDA: I think you should.

MISSY: So are you thinking of applying for the US schools?

AMANDA: I'd love to.

MISSY: You're definitely talented enough… But the trouble is, a fair few people are. And there's only so many places.

AMANDA: And scholarships.

Beat.

Are you jealous?

MISSY: Of..?

AMANDA: Toni. That she got to go.

MISSY: Sometimes.

Beat.

AMANDA: Do you miss her?

MISSY: I did...

AMANDA: She was so good, at school. I used to look up to her and want to be as good as her! And you actually!

MISSY: You don't have to say that.

AMANDA: I'm being honest!

MISSY: That's nice to hear.

AMANDA: I think cos Toni was a forward I noticed her first...

MISSY: She is so talented.

AMANDA: You worked well together, on the team...

MISSY: You know, the first week she FaceTimed me every day.

AMANDA: Will you get to go out and see her?

MISSY: No. I think that ship has definitely sailed.

AMANDA: Ah!

MISSY: I think she's met someone new. Her instagram is popping off. You know when people are like "look I've got someone new now". I don't know if they do it on purpose...

AMANDA: So cringe, why do people do that?

MISSY: It is cringe isn't it?

AMANDA: Maybe you and me should take a photo together and be like best day ever playing football...

MISSY: Ha. Maybe... Maybe after we win?

AMANDA: Yeah, smashing this match will make you feel better. It always does for me.

MISSY: I think you could be right.

Beat.

AMANDA: Erm. Shirt colour?

MISSY: Gold!

AMANDA: They're definitely yellow.

Enter **LEXI.**

LEXI: You two look a bit ally pally … Everything alright?

MISSY: Yeah course.

AMANDA: We're just gonna teach our new fans a chant weren't we Miss?

MISSY: Oh yeah! Of course.

AMANDA: Okay everyone, so it goes RM13, RM13 when I say Rainham you say WHAT, Rainham – WHAT, Rainham WHAT!

A, L, M: RM13, RM13 when I say Rainham you say WHAT. Rainham

AUDIENCE: WHAT

A, L, M: Rainham

AUDIENCE: WHAT.

SCENE 5 (III):

Misha's Team

The Influencer

AUDIENCE: PINK WRISTBANDS

LOCATION: DUG OUTS

CHARACTERS: SCRAPPY, ELLIE MAE

SCRAPPY: Alright?

ELLIE: Oh hey!

SCRAPPY: What you doing?

ELLIE: Just setting up for a shoot, you?

SCRAPPY: Penalty shoot out?

ELLIE: No, a photoshoot. I'm an influencer.

SCRAPPY: Oh sick. You got bare followers then?

ELLIE: Yeah, like 30K.

SCRAPPY: Woah. I've got 216.

ELLIE: That's still good.

SCRAPPY: Ah, you think?

ELLIE: Well, no, but I was being polite.

SCRAPPY: You're a decent footballer though, init. Your followers all football fans or…?

ELLIE: Yeah mostly. My most liked video is me doing a cross bar challenge for James Milner. I hit it first time and he says "beginner's luck". The fans loved it.

SCRAPPY: Wow.

ELLIE: He's not as boring as people say…

SCRAPPY: Milner?

ELLIE: Okay, he is well boring, I was just being nice.

SCRAPPY: So you're training with us tonight, for the scout?

ELLIE: Yep. My agent thinks getting on a team will be good for the gram, and equally I'll be good for the team.

SCRAPPY: Yeah great. Well I have this lot with me, do you think they can help with your shoot?

ELLIE: Yeah definitely. I'm gonna film a YouTube vid, if they wanna help. Find a seat and quiet on set.

SCRAPPY: Once you're done, we'll see you in front of the away stand!

ELLIE: I'm obviously anticipating being scouted by Dagenham & Redbridge women's so I'm just gonna do it as if I've already been asked, okay?

Get your phones out then. Then my followers can become your followers and vice versa. Don't forget to hashtag Squad Goals. Tag your location. You know the drill. Okay, ready?

Hi everyone, Ellie-Mae here, welcome to my channel. Today I'd like to talk to you about sports. I've recently been offered a place on a brand new women's football team which is super exciting for me as a female footballer. I was so inspired by the recent Women's World Cup and I'm ready to document my time for you all as part of this new team.

First things first. The shirt. Such a big fan of the colour. Obviously you can't go wrong with a Nike sports shirt! We've got the logo right here, and the number on the back! It's a sleek, cool design, which I think says a lot about the girls on my team and hopefully how we play football.

Hairstyles, I've opted for the front back, off my face. There is nothing worse than a windy day and hair flying in your face. Not a good look. I've left the back loose and sprayed with BLEACH Swamp Spritz beach waves spray.

Make-up, I've used my everyday make-up tutorial – The link is in my bio.

I will be posting teasers from our training sessions on my instagram every day throughout the season so you can follow our progress – so don't forget to follow me on there too.

As always I'll keep you updated! Thank you for watching. And make sure you support Dagenham & Redbridge FC.

Okay perfect. I'm a one take wonder, right? Let's see if we can get some decent content anywhere else in this ground… Maybe in the tunnel?

SCENE FIVE (IV):

Misha's Team

I'm Sharky

AUDIENCE: PINK WRISTBANDS

LOCATION: CORNER OF AWAY STAND & CARLING STAND

CHARACTERS: SHARKY

A goal is chalked out on the wall.

SHARKY: Right. Who fancies themselves as a bit of a footballer then?
Maybe I'll pick one of ya to take a couple of shots… Great, so incase
any of you are the scout, you've probably guessed I'm not local talent.
But, let me make my claim, back home, there's not really a footie
scene. I always come down and stay with Scraps. I'm at college up
North, but colleges are super laid back aren't they? Like, you don't
need to go in every day and that. I've heard that's what uni is like too.
I'd like to go to uni, but don't really know what the deal is with what
I'd do there? Did any of you go to uni? What did you study? Do you
think that'd be good for me? But yeah, I've gone off track… If any of
you are the scout, I'd love to be given the opportunity. I can show you
how good I am, right?

Okay, who fancies a couple of shots.

Audience members can take a couple of shots against **SHARKY**.

I'm a bit nervous about this whole thing, if I do get picked I'd have to
move down here, and Scrappy's flat doesn't really have the room…
There's no money in the women's game yet really is there? So I'd have
to find a proper job down here as well… It's a lot to think about.

Enter **ASSASSINA**, *she steps up and takes a shot against* **SHARKY**.

ASSASSINA: Ciao!

SHARKY: Assassina! How are you, mate? Long time no see!

ASSASSINA: I am good thank you! I'm here to play. I heard there's a
scout?

SHARKY: Oh yes! I'll go & grab Scraps and we'll go through everything with ya. Gang, can you keep Assassina entertained for a bit. She's a legend, so make her feel welcome and obviously she's European so maybe don't mention Brexit?

ASSASSINA: Ciao, ciao. Nice to meet you all. Are you all football fans or..? Great. If you're not already, you will be after you've watched me on the pitch. Apparently there's a game happening in a bit?

So how are the English at football? Have you heard of a, erm, what do you call it? A nutmeg? Yes I will nutmeg you. And a sliding tackle? I'll do that too. BUT, if you want to support me, I will do both your team and my country proud. So when I get the ball we could try some encouraging words in Italian, erm how about forza! – That means "go on"… Forza Assassina!

Everyone – Here's the chant

Forza, Forza Assassina!

Forza, Forza Assassina!

Yes! Sounds perfect. Okay I'm off to erm… what's it called? Put more hair gel in my ponytail, and I'll see you all in a bit.

The audience are all together from this point on. Each character from Scene Five will lead their audience back into the away stand.

SCENE SIX (I):

He's a boy

AUDIENCE: BLUE & PINK WRISTBANDS

LOCATION: AWAY STAND

CHARACTERS: AMANDA, MEL, MISSY, SHANE, LEXI

ENTER MEL *&* **SHANE**

MISSY: *(to **AMANDA** & audience)* Watch this.

MEL: Guys, this is Shane.

SHANE: Hello.

MISSY *switches to huge comedy flirt.*

MISSY: Hello you.

AMANDA *giggles.*

LEXI: Shane?

MEL: Shane.

LEXI: Right.

SHANE: I sold Mel the Skoda.

LEXI: Oh!

MISSY: Nice to meet you, Shane.

MEL: Shane's a footballer.

LEXI: Great,

MISSY: What a coincidence, so am I.

SHANE: Cool.

MISSY: I'm also a lawyer.

LEXI: Undergrad.

SHANE: Still cool.

AMANDA: So is Shane here to play football?

MISSY: Good for eye candy, aren't you sweetheart?

LEXI: Stop it.

MEL: I thought he might be a good addition to the team.

AMANDA: Of course.

MEL: Shane –

SHANE: Hi.

LEXI: It's a shame he's a he.

MEL: Obviously.

MISSY: Quite obviously a he.

LEXI: Stop it.

SHANE: Nice to meet you all.

MEL: He played for West Ham U15!

AMANDA: Oh sick.

SHANE: – before my injury.

MISSY: Ooh, East London boy!

LEXI: Where do we sign?

MEL: There we go!

MISSY: I'll draw you up a contract... I can do that because I'm a lawyer.

LEXI: In all seriousness, we need to beat Misha. And if ex-Hammers here can do that, I'm okay with it.

SHANE: Wait, we? I don't see any men?

He looks around. The space is full of women. It's a duh moment.

Oh no.

AMANDA: So is that a yes?

They all pout & pull puppy dog eyes.

SHANE: What are you all doing?

MEL: Being cute.

SHANE: Okay, I'll play if you stop making those faces.

LEXI: Amazing! Let's get ourselves a match!

SCENE SIX (II):

Ellie-Mae

AUDIENCE: BLUE & PINK WRISTBANDS

LOCATION: AWAY STAND

CHARACTERS: MISHA, SHARKY, SCRAPPY, ELLIE-MAE

MISHA: The official line is "Amanda has decided to part ways with us".

SHARKY: Oh no!

SCRAPPY: Good riddance!

SHARKY: Yeah, do one!

MISHA: So we have our 'high-profile' Italian transfer to announce…

SHARKY: She's here, wait, where's she gone? I left her with you lot!

Oh okay. She's gelling her hair. But we still need one more player?

SCRAPPY: Quick maths! And I found her!

ELLIE: Hello!

SHARKY: Oh! She's well pretty.

MISHA: She doesn't need to be pretty. Can you play football?

SCRAPPY: Have you not seen her Instagram?! She's got loads of pictures with footballs.

MISHA: Right.

SHARKY: So by association she's a footballer.

ELLIE: I can definitely play football

SHARKY: I think you're so pretty.

ELLIE: You and 30,000 other people.

SCRAPPY: Is that how many followers you've got?

ELLIE: And counting!

MISHA: So I'm Misha. Player-manager…

ELLIE: Thanks for asking me to join.

MISHA: Oh I –

ELLIE: I assume it's you my agent invoices then?

MISHA: Agent? Invoices? Wait, no, we're just… it's a community project… for fun…

ELLIE: Huh?

MISHA: Yeah no one gets paid.

ELLIE: So you're not the scout?

SCRAPPY : We thought you'd do it for the likes?

SHARKY: Do it for the likes, Ellie.

ELLIE: Women's football is so in right now.

And actually with my presence, we could in fact make some money out of it… branded advertisements… sporty women… strong not skinny…

MISHA: Can you play though?

ELLIE: I did a cross bar challenge with James Milner – I can send you the link?

SCRAPPY: I've JUST seen it… she hits it, first try!

SHARKY: I've seen that – she hits it, first try.

SCRAPPY: Milner says "beginner's luck" and laughs.

SHARKY: *(laughs)* – He laughs!

SCRAPPY: We should let her play.

SHARKY: Please… I don't get to meet women like this in Halifax.

ELLIE: Thank you?

MISHA: Okay. You're on trial. Welcome to the squad.

ELLIE: Selfie! Timer! Three seconds. Hashtag Squad Goals

The group gather to get a selfie.

SCENE SEVEN:

Match

AUDIENCE: PINK & BLUE WRISTBANDS

LOCATION: AWAY STAND

CHARACTERS: ALL

Enter **ASSASSINA**.

ASSASSINA: I'm so excited to be trialling for an English league, after growing up watching the likes of Steven Gerrard, Frank Lampard and David Beckham. You know as a kid everyone wants to play for a team like this, so I am grateful and honoured to be able to play in the UK. My family are really excited to visit the ground, and I know I'm going to make them proud. It has been a tough journey that has led me here.

SCRAPPY: Ryan Air?

ASSASSINA: Si.

But I'm excited to train with these talented women.

SHARKY: Assassina! What would you say your best attributes are as a player?

ASSASSINA: Dribbling, speed, tackling… Shooting, scoring.

SCRAPPY: Really talented,

MISHA: Apparently so!

SCRAPPY: We're excited to have you with us.

SHARKY: Assassina! How do you feel about your player-manager Misha?

ASSASSINA: I mean, we've spoken through what her plans for me would be this season.

MISHA: We're giving nothing away.

ELLIE: Girls, who is this for?

SCRAPPY: What?

ELLIE: I mean what are we doing right now?

SCRAPPY: It can be for your YouTube channel.

SHARKY: For the fans.

ELLIE: Right –

Beat.

Do we have fans?

SHARKY: No

SCRAPPY: Loads.

SHARKY: Yeah. Loads.

ELLIE: Wow.

MISHA: Our fans are any female identifying individual who feels like they're not allowed to reach their full potential as a human. Actually anyone who has felt restricted or oppressed by gender stereotypes and trying to be "the norm" or what's expected.

SCRAPPY: Kill the men.

ELLIE: Woah, feminism isn't about killing men!

SHARKY: That's a shame. I had my heart broken the last day I was in Halifax.

ELLIE: I'm sorry to hear that.

SHARKY: So can we kill them?

ELLIE: No. We need them to be allies and support us. Ah! Tweeting it!

MISHA: They don't want the status quo to change though.

SCRAPPY: Kill 'em.

ELLIE: No.

SCRAPPY: The next man I'm gonna see, I'm gonna kill.

*Enter **LEXI**'s team.*

SHANE: Hello!

SCRAPPY *growls and launches herself at* **SHANE**, **ELLIE** *grabs her and restrains her.*

    You okay, hun?

MISHA: What are you doing here?

AMANDA: Got a team together didn't I?

LEXI: I think I got the team together, but minor details.

ELLIE: Sounds fun!

MISHA: You lot wanna play us?

SHARKY: Do you have a boy on your team?

MISSY: A man.

MEL: Yeah and what?

MISHA: He won't be able to play against us?

AMANDA: Why not?

SCRAPPY: Cos it ain't the rules.

LEXI: Whose rules, your mum's?

MISHA: You better shut up.

SHARKY: Yeah.

AMANDA: You scared?

SHARKY: Yeah

MISHA: Scared of what?

SCRAPPY: Scared of a boy?

SHARKY: Yeah.

MEL: Yeah!

SHARKY: Pfft. No we're not… Are we?

MISHA: No we're not.

SCRAPPY: I'm scared.

SHARKY: Oh?

SCRAPPY: Scared I'll get sent off when I hack him down.

LEXI: So you will play us?

MISHA: Why not?

ASSASSINA: Let's see what you've got –

SHARKY: If you think you're all that.

MISSY: Who are you? I've not seen you round here before?

ASSASSINA: Assassina

SCRAPPY *&* **SHARKY** *do the whip crack sound effect together.*

SCRAPPY: It means murderer in Eye-talian

SHARKY: Have you actually killed someone?

ASSASSINA: A lady never tells.

SHARKY: Wow.

SHANE: Crap.

LEXI: Not crap! – We're the stronger team. We'll prove it.

AMANDA: You asked me for a match and here we are.

LEXI: Unless you're worried I'll be picked by the scout over you?

MISHA: Shouldn't you be home studying for your A Levels?

LEXI: At least some of us are clever enough to do A Levels, how's your BTEC coming along?

MEL: Oi Lex, I'm on a BTEC

LEXI: Oops sorry.

MISHA: Doesn't bother me, I know I've got a bright career ahead of me cos I work hard.

ELLIE: Just FYI, grades overall mean nothing, I was obviously screwed over by the government with my A Levels so I decided to pursue fame and fortune and look at me…

They look at her.

I'm doing great.

MEL: Hmm don't know how helpful that info is but sure.

MISSY: Oh my god, I thought I recognised you!

ELLIE: @ EllieMaeHague

MISSY: I love your insta!

ELLIE: Aww thanks baby gal. I'll follow you back, what's yours.

MISSY: LilMissyxox

LEXI: Seriously?

AMANDA: So are we playing or what?

MISHA: The match sounds great.

SCRAPPY: We'll be bringing it.

SHARKY: Yeah.

MISHA: Got a team name?

LEXI: Erm…

MEL: Rainham Wanderers.

SCRAPPY: And we'll be the Dagenham Daggers!

MEL: Dagenham's nickname is already Daggers.

SCRAPPY: Yeah, and?

MEL: It's like you're saying Dagenham twice.

MISHA: What's it matter? – We know you ain't fit enough to beat us so…

LEXI: So we're even then?

MISHA: What do you mean?

LEXI: You know my weakness is fitness…

MISHA: What?

LEXI: I know your weakness is no one wanted to play with you at school.

MEL: Lexi –

LEXI: Cos you're a bully.

MISHA: You better shut up.

LEXI: Yeah. Didn't the boys reject you off of their team? And even the girls didn't really wanna play with you after that fiasco…

MISHA: It was Mr. Evans who wanted me on the boys team, not me.

LEXI: And your mum?

AMANDA: Leave it, Lex.

MISHA: Yeah leave it Lex. Cos I made captain at Harris and you didn't… And your team consists of one of our rejects, your next door neighbour, your failed footballer of a sister and a random boy.

SHANE: Random?

MISHA'S MUM V/O: The matches will begin in fifteen minutes. That's fifteen minutes to get your teams registered girls.

SCRAPPY: See you in fifteen

MISHA: Rainham Rejects.

SHARKY: Rejects! Good one.

MISHA's **TEAM** *exit through the tunnel laughing*

SHANE: I need a beer! Where's the bar?

MEL: Why don't you lot all grab a beer and take a seat? The match will start in fifteen mins. C'mon Hammers!

SFX: Level Up – Ciara

59

Act 2

SCENE 1

The Match

A thirty min danced football match.

AUDIENCE: BLUE & PINK WRISTBANDS

LOCATION: 5-A-SIDE PITCH *(IN FRONT OF AWAY STAND)*

CHARACTERS: ALL

First Half – Fifteen mins

(The "ball" should definitely always be the main focus, but moments should happen with & between other characters when they're not on the ball. The moments laid out here are total guidelines, more passes / tackles should be made within each section so it is fast paced, but the main plot of play is written here.)

Opens with running out the tunnel [Missy Elliott's Badman]

Kick off – **MISHA**'s team kick off cos they're at "home" [whistle blows]

MISHA & **SCRAPPY-DOO** start central and kick off.

Ball is played between **MISHA** & **SCRAPPY**, they are TERRIFYING.

LEXI has a couple of tackles.

The ball is passed from **MISHA** to **SCRAPPY** to **ELLIE** to **ASSASSINA**, Cristiano Ronaldo style step overs, back to **ELLIE**, back to **ASSASSINA** [Jucee Froot's Danger]

ASSASSINA has a shot. Saved. Rainham with a uniformed moment of relief and celebrating **MEL** saving the shot [Anne-Marie's Ciao Adios]

MEL kicks the ball back into play, to **LEXI** [on last "I'm done"]

LEXI has her chance for Ronaldinho style keepie uppies and general show-boating. [Pussycat Doll's When I Grow Up]

LEXI passes to **AMANDA**, **AMANDA** is tackled by **SCRAPPY-DOO**. **SCRAPPY** has a shot from their half of the pitch, it flies over the net, naturally.

MISHA tells **SCRAPPY** off.

MEL kicks it back into play, this time to **SHANE**, he goes head to head with **ASSASSINA** as she attempts to take it off him. [Dua Lipa's Physical]

MISSY comes to **SHANE**'s rescue, she's too COOL, she is on the ball and can't be stopped. Didn't get that scholarship, WHAT? cos she's sick. She shoots.

GOAL!

They all become **MISSY**'s backing dancers [Doja Cat's Boss Bitch]

MISSY to **LEXI** to **AMANDA**, SHOT! [a breath of silence]

GOAL! [Spice Girl's Spice Up Your Life]

Rainham celebrate.

Ball back to centre for Dagenham kick off [Little Mix's Bounce Back]

Dagenham keeps possession, it's frustrating for the Rainham players.

SCRAPPY terrorises **SHANE**.

ASSASSINA is able to show off.

SCRAPPY toe punts a terrible misplaced pass into the stands.

ALL PLAYERS: Woooooah!

ELLIE-MAE hits the cross bar, it bounces back into play.

Rainham break with **AMANDA** on the ball.

AMANDA gets her moment to show off. [Shakira's Hips Don't Lie]

She takes a shot and misses.

SHARKY kicks the ball back into play.

Big group movement section – they are having fun, everyone really wants to be next to score. [Taylor Swift's Shake It Off]

SFX: Whistle blows

SCENE 2 (I)

Misha's team

Half Time Chat

AUDIENCE: BLUE & PINK WRISTBANDS

LOCATION: 5-A-SIDE PITCH

CHARACTERS: MISHA, SCRAPPY DOO, SHARKY, ASSASSINA & ELLIE

SHARKY: I'm sorry! I'm so, so sorry!

SCRAPPY: You're not the one who should be apologising.

MISHA: Happens to the best of us.

SHARKY: She came out of nowhere. She's fast.

ELLIE: Yeah, no one could've saved that first one.

SHARKY: Talking of saves, Assassina, if you'd put that shot away we wouldn't be so far behind.

MISHA: That's generally how it works –

ASSASSINA: What did you say to me?

SHARKY: If. You'd. Put. That. Shot. Away…

SCRAPPY: – Naa! She means, that keeper had a lucky save.

SHARKY: Lucky?

ELLIE: She is well good, their keeper!

SHARKY: What you trying to say?

ELLIE: No nothing…

SCRAPPY: Amanda is good, I don't know why we ever let her go?

MISHA: We don't need her.

SCRAPPY: Don't we Misha?

SHARKY: We should've signed that keeper too.

ELLIE: That's reassuring coming from our actual keeper.

SHARKY: Oh yeah.

MISHA: Please stop –

SCRAPPY: What's happened to you?

MISHA: What?

SCRAPPY: You lost your head in that mate.

ASSASSINA: I didn't fly all the way over here to lose to "lucky" goals. I cannot be average here! My parents are watching.

MISHA: Join the club!!

ASASSINA: You see, I come from a country of some of the best footballers in the world. Four world cup wins.

SHARKY: What about your women's team though?

ASSASSINA: We had some hard games last year!

ELLIE: Google says only fifteenth best in the world.

ASSASSINA: Numbers mean nothing!

SHARKY: England Women's are third.

ASSASSINA: And yet you English are still holding on to '66.

MISHA: Girls, can we focus?

SCRAPPY: You focus.

MISHA: I am focused.

ASSASSINA: We're getting totally murdered in the middle,

SCRAPPY: Which is Lexi. Why aren't you marking her Meesh?

MISHA: I am –

SCRAPPY: Naa, you're out of it.

ASSASSINA: I thought you were supposed to be the best around here?

SCRAPPY: What's your mum gonna say after? Think about it!

MISHA: Probably that I'm playing bad... I don't care...

SCRAPPY: She's set all this up for you.

MISHA: She's set all this up for her more like.

SCRAPPY: For your future, you have the best chance out of all of us –

MISHA: – I literally don't care

SHARKY: What do you mean you don't care?

ELLIE: I thought you eat, sleep and breathe football?

SCRAPPY: She does, this is ridiculous

MISHA: You're ridiculous.

SCRAPPY: Tell us what is going on?

MISHA: I don't wanna play anymore, alright!?!

   Beat.

SCRAPPY: What?

MISHA: I don't wanna do it anymore.

SCRAPPY: Why?

MISHA: I've loved it. I do love it.

SCRAPPY: I know you do.

MISHA: I've been working weekends in a beauty salon

SCRAPPY: WHAT THE ACTUAL –

MISHA: As an apprentice.

   The girls think she's joking.

MISHA: Don't laugh. I love it. I wanna do that instead. I wanna be an
   eyelash technician or something...

SCRAPPY: Naa you're having us on.

MISHA: You shouldn't be laughing. You should be championing me. If
   you were my mates...

SCRAPPY: You're joking?

MISHA: I'm not, Scraps.

SHARKY: Aww. That is quite nice actually.

MISHA: After today I'm hanging up my boots. I'm gonna tell my mum tonight.

SCRAPPY: Wow.

ELLIE: Are you sure?

MISHA: So sure.

SCRAPPY: But –

MISHA: – No buts, I love my new job, I wanna concentrate on getting all my training…

SCRAPPY: And that's what makes you happy?

MISHA: One hundred percent.

SCRAPPY: Well. Then I say, let's give you a cracking final testimonial match.

ASSASSINA: Girls as nice as this all is, following your dreams and all, my dream is still football and I came here to WIN.

MISHA: Great! The pressure is off! I'm changing up the formation. Assassina is our weapon, and we must use her as such. We'll put her up against the boy, and that should give us a chance to take this game back. Let's get ready!

SCENE 2 (II)

Lexi's team

Half Time Chat

AUDIENCE: BLUE & PINK WRISTBANDS

LOCATION: 5-A-SIDE PITCH

CHARACTERS: LEXI, MEL, AMANDA, SHANE, MISSY

LEXI: Some great shots, Amanda! We just can't get carried away now.

AMANDA: So true!

MISSY: Amazing save, Mel.

MEL: Surprised myself, you know!

LEXI: Best female goalie.

SHANE: Girls. You're all amazing.

MEL: We prefer 'women'.

SHANE: Of course. You're all amazing.

MISSY: I am a woman of many talents –

LEXI: I think they may have spotted our weakness.

SHANE: Where is that?

The girls clench their teeth and look at **SHANE**.

AMANDA: I think they'll look to change formation.

LEXI: Yes. It looks like you'll be marking Assassina this half, Shane.

SHANE: The murderer? So first the scary girl – woman and now the murderer?

LEXI: We believe in you.

AMANDA: What's wrong with Misha?

LEXI: She's lost her head, mate.

AMANDA: You keep getting past her.

LEXI: It's weird cos she knows all my tricks. She's definitely off her game.

AMANDA: Chance for you to have a couple of shots second half then.

LEXI: Buzzing.

MEL: I just wanna take this moment to say I'm having the best day with you all. I'm so glad we disobeyed your mum and stayed to play football. I don't even care how much trouble we get into!

Beat.

LEXI: O-K… So. If in doubt, pass to Amanda. Their goalie is weak.

AMANDA: To the tunnel!

ALL *exit except* **LEXI** *&* **MISSY**.

MISSY: Sis, can I talk to you?

LEXI: Yeah? What's up? You all good with the changes?

MISSY: Oh yeah, course… I just wanted to say I'm really proud of you, and that scout would be mad to not pick you after today.

LEXI: Ah what? Stop it!

MISSY: I mean it. I want you to know…

I spoke to Amanda earlier.

LEXI: Oh god you fancy her don't you?

MISSY: What? No! I mean… Well, I'm not sure but –

LEXI: – For god's sake.

MISSY: No I'm trying to tell you something important!

LEXI: What is it?

MISSY: The university of Central Florida Soccer Programme.

LEXI: I know, I'm sorry –

MISSY: – I had a place with a full scholarship.

LEXI: What? Why haven't you gone?

MISSY: Because –

LEXI: – I'm so mad with you. Why wouldn't you take that opportunity?

MISSY: Listen. That isn't my path anymore. Things happen for a reason. I made the decision and I'm happy with it.

LEXI: So why are you telling me now?

MISSY: I wanted you to know girls from round here can do whatever they set their minds too.

LEXI: You're a sick player Missy. All I could think in that first half is how sick you are. I hope I'm even half as good as you sis.

MISSY: You are better than me, Lex. And I believe in you whole-heartedly.

LEXI: I love you, you know. I still want your bedroom as a walk in wardrobe, but I do love you.

MISSY: I love you, crazy kid. Now, win the match, set me up with your friend and we can all go home happy.

LEXI: To the tunnel?

MISSY: To the tunnel.

SCENE THREE:

The Match

2nd Half

AUDIENCE: BLUE & PINK WRISTBANDS

LOCATION: 5-A-SIDE PITCH *(IN FRONT OF AWAY STAND)*

CHARACTERS: ALL

Second Half – Fifteen mins.

They swap ends.

They run out of the tunnel [JLo's Let's Get Loud, layered again with vu vu zelas, whistles, cheering, etc etc]

Rainham kick-off.

The ball ping pongs.

Everyone gets a moment to show off.

SCRAPPY gets nut-megged by **SHANE**, we see her expression change, she slide tackles – something bookable, if she was a wild animal she would be peacocking/sharpening her claws or horns [K.Flay's Bad Memory]

Ref gets involved, splits them up.

Yellow card.

Free kick to Rainham, they let **SHANE** take it. [Megan Thee Stallion's Savage]

Dagenham makes a wall, they're doing what they can to put him off.

The ball flies over the crossbar.

Dagenham dance, united in their celebration.

SHARKY kicks the ball back into play. [Ariana Grande's Focus]

The ball ping pongs.

Tackles all over the place.

A couple of naff shots.

Ends with **SCRAPPY** having a shot.

[Lizzo's Juice]

GOAL!

Dagenham celebrate.

[Beyonce's Formation]

Possession is kept by Dagenham, Rainham have a couple of tackles. Dagenham are showing off.

AMANDA gets the ball, showboats. If **LEXI** is Ronaldinho, **AMANDA** is Lionel Messi. Dagenham try and block her [Britney Spear's Toxic Remix]

ELLIE tackles. Her solo. Everyone becomes her backing dancers. Ends with her taking a shot, it hits the cross bar bounces back into play **ASSASSINA** heads it in [Girls Aloud's Sound of the Underground. Use the intro but jump to the last chorus]

GOAL!

Dagenham celebrate! [Saweetie & GALXARA's Sway With Me]

LEXI & **AMANDA** kick off. [Ciara feat. Kelly Rowland's Girl Gang]

The ball ping pongs, changing possession.

MISHA fouls **LEXI**.

LEXI penalty [Hit Me with your Best Shot – Adona]

She steps up.

The world moves in slow motion.

GOAL!

They celebrate.

Final minute of play, the girls are having fun now. [Little Mix – Wings]

SFX: Whistle is blown

MISHA'S MUM V/O: FINAL SCORE: 3-2 to Rainham

SCENE 4

LEXI & *Rainham celebrate, they shake hands with Dagenham.*

During this **LEXI** *talks to a match official.*

SWING: Lexi! I've just spoken to the scout. They want you for a trial at
  Dagenham & Redbridge women's.

LEXI: Naa, you're joking.

SWING: I'm not! Seriously well done Lex, you smashed it.

  Beat.

LEXI: Oh my god. Shut up.

  I've got a trial at Dagenham & Redbridge –

MISSY: What?

LEXI: Yeah from the scout, I've got a trial!

SCRAPPY: What is it? What's happened.

MISSY: She's got a trial at Dagenham!

The ball is thrown in the air in celebration. It is caught by **MISHA.**

LEXI: Ah I'm sorry Misha.

MISHA: Naa, fair play Lexi. Well deserved.

SCRAPPY: And you're gonna be alright ain't ya Meesh?

MISHA: Ah that reminds me. Mum… I don't wanna do it anymore. I've got a job I love … it's in beauty … and I'm happy.

Throws ball in the air. It is caught by **SCRAPPY.**

SCRAPPY: I'm just buzzing a local girl has got to take the chance. Maybe if I hadn't played so dirty, it would've been me. Put a good word in for me for next season, Lex?

Throws ball in the air. It is caught by **SHANE.**

SHANE: Gutted it wasn't me who got scouted. Just kidding. But seriously what an amazing group of girls.

The **WOMEN** *cough.*

SHANE: Oops! Women. Lex so well deserved, you're a sick player. And the best news is – I SOLD MY SKODA!

Had a right laugh with you all today – Same time tomorrow?

Throws ball in the air. It is caught by **ASSASSINA.**

ASSASSINA: Well done Lexi. I've had the best holiday ever playing with you all. The English do have talent apparently! Don't get too complacent, I'll be back before you know it and I'll need a fresh challenge.

Throws ball in the air. It is caught by **AMANDA.**

AMANDA: Those chicken legs actually paid off. Well done Lex. So proud of you. And Miss?

MISSY: Yeah?

AMANDA: Fancy a cheeky bev?

Throws ball to **MISSY.**

MISSY: Go on then! My sister gets to live her dreams and I've bagged a girlfriend. I am a woman who gets what she wants after all!

Throws ball in the air. It is caught by **SHARKY**.

SHARKY: Oh balls to it. Who thinks I should stay in Daggers?

Who's got a spare room?

Beat.

SCRAPPY: You've always got a bed at mine Sharks!

Throws ball in the air. It is caught by **ELLIE-MAE**.

ELLIE: I'm actually really quite taken with you all… My algorithm has improved since you've all appeared on my stories… I'm almost famous enough to be on Love Island!

Beat.

I'm actually just really happy I found a group of girl mates. I've never had this before. I think I'll stick around.

Throws ball in the air. It is caught by **MEL**.

She cuddles it and stares to the audience.

MEL: I've had the best day! It seems everything turned out alright in the end.

LEXI: Well if it ain't alright it ain't the end?

MEL: Proud of you bestie.

SFX: Let's Get Loud.

A celebratory movement section begins, incorporating bows. Audience are encouraged to film / take photos for this last section.

LEXI: Thank you so much for supporting us today! Obviously times are hard for sport at the moment!

MEL: And for the arts!

MISHA: So please do if you've enjoyed your time at *Squad Goals* post about us on social media and tell your friends!

MEL: Hopefully see you again soon!

Cast all wave & run down the tunnel.

SFX: Let's Get Loud – play out

END.